MW01598694

The Phenological Fly

A METHOD *for* MEETING *and* MATCHING
the SUPER HATCHES *of the* WEST

Bob Scammell

 Blue Ribbon Books

JOHNSON GORMAN PUBLISHERS

BLUE RIBBON BOOKS ARE PUBLISHED BY
Johnson Gorman Publishers Ltd.
3669 – 41 Avenue
Red Deer Alberta Canada T4N 5H5

Design by Full Court Press.
Printed and bound in Canada by D.W. Friesen Ltd.
for Johnson Gorman Publishers.

ACKNOWLEDGEMENTS
Financial support provided by the Alberta Foundation for the Arts, a beneficiary of the Lottery Fund of the Government of Alberta.

  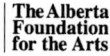 

COMMITTED TO THE DEVELOPMENT OF CULTURE AND THE ARTS

CANADIAN CATALOGUING IN PUBLICATION DATA
Scammell, Robert, 1937–
The phenological fly
Blue Ribbon Books
ISBN 0-921835-15-9
1. Fly fishing.   2. Insects—Identification.   I. Title.
SH456.S32   1995   799.1'2   C95-910228-0

6 5 4 3 2 1

COVER: Bastard Adams and Brown Drake on Heart-leaved Arnica (*Arnica cordifolia*)

CONTENTS

Golden Stone on wild rose (Rosa acicularis)

I

INTRODUCTION

THE REVOLUTION of the eighties for fly-fishers was their discovery that something called aquatic entomology exists in western North America. The decade revealed that we in Alberta, British Columbia, Montana, Idaho and other points west have hatches every bit as super as anything the East offers, even the legendary and misnamed giant Mayfly, the Michigan Caddis *(Hexagenia limbata)*. Our formerly rough and ready western fly-fishing has been refined by knowledge of our own important insect hatches.

For the purposes of this book, a super hatch is the emergence of an aquatic insect from its underwater to its adult, flying form that triggers major feeding in major fish, particularly trout. Essential to making the emergence a super hatch are factors such as sheer numbers of insects, their size, habits that make them vulnerable to fish, and intangibles to humans, such as flavor. In short, a super hatch is fly-fishing at its best because it produces super feeding for the trout and super fishing for the angler.

I include among super hatch insects our smallest Mayfly, *Tricorythodes*, known to anglers as Tricos, because it is an aquatic insect that hatches in the billions and that trout gulp by the mouthful, but I exclude the annual plague of grasshoppers and the super fishing it triggers because the grasshopper is a terrestrial insect that only appears on the water by accident or when there is a grasshopper wind.

Most Caddisflies are also excluded, except the Fall Caddis as a possible super hatch. I concede that Caddis generally can be important hatches, being the cause of many evening rises. But, because they are hard to identify with certainty and hard to photograph because of their hyperactivity and perpetual motion, they remain my project for the 21st century.

Few fly-fishers, wherever they live, know much about the fabled super hatches. When they take place (including time of year, time of day and type of weather), what the insects look like (especially to an angler astream without magnifying glass, let alone scientific keys to identification) and how the insects behave and how best to imitate them are a mystery to most.

Even anglers who have experienced the heaven of having stumbled onto a super hatch in progress and enjoyed exceptional fishing seem unable to make the connections that will enable them to repeat the experience the next year. Few modern anglers keep a fishing diary, that faithful repository of lore that guided pioneer fly-fishers in England and Eastern North America. In fairness, most experts readily admit that meeting hatches year after year is very difficult because of the many variables that contribute to their timing. Rick Hafele, entomology columnist for *American Angler* magazine, explores some of these variables and resulting difficulties in his March/April 1994 column titled "Catching Hatches: Easier Said Than Done!" Other than genetics and food supply, Hafele notes water temperature and photoperiod (number of hours of daylight per day) as the principal factors driving the timing of hatches.

What we are seeing in the nineties is a resort to technology, to the instant solutions of hatch and river hotlines, computer programs, newsletters and informal networks of anglers with cellular phones in their rigs. The problems with these substitutes for real knowledge derived from observation and experience—in other words, from lore—are that they do not take account of the variables, and, worse, they lead to the malaise of modern fly-fishing: everyone going to all the same places at the same time. Technological substitutes also lead to the misconception in new fly-fishers that these are the only places to fish a super hatch, and thus they miss entirely the personal voyages of discovery that used to form the early part of every angler's apprenticeship. In most parts of western North America it is still possible to discover new places and private super hatches of the usual insects or, perhaps, as has happened to me in entomologically unexplored Alberta, the discovery of an entirely new super hatch of an insect not previously known by anglers to exist in a region.

2

THE PHENOLOGY
SOLUTION

THE TRICK to entering fly-fishers' heaven is being present when a super hatch is occurring. In this book I offer a method for achieving just that, a method arising from the ancient science of phenology. Phenology is derived from the Greek *phaino*, meaning to appear. Thus it is the science of appearances, and it has many uses. For me, one of these involves making a connection between the appearances of aquatic insects and wildflowers—specifically, connecting the appearance, or flowering, of certain streamside wildflowers to the appearance, or hatch, of those insects that form the super hatches so interesting to both fish and anglers.

Phenology, though I did not always recognize it as such, has been a preoccupation throughout my angling life. When I was a kid in what was then not known as trout country, signs and portents were distilled into wise sayings to guide what fishing we had: "Pickerel (that's what they call Walleye in southern Alberta) run when the Cottonwood blooms and blows;" "Goldeye run when the wild roses bloom." Old wives' tales perhaps, but anglers ignored them at their angling peril.

Later, I moved to central Alberta's prime trout country and

eventually noticed, without first thinking much about it, that wild roses were also blooming when the Golden Stonefly hatch was on and, earlier, Dogwood flowers were just starting to bud when the Salmonflies emerged on my favorite stream. Eventually and fortuitously, I became a volunteer field observer for the Alberta Wildflower Survey, a phenological project that started in 1973 and now involves reporting the flowering dates of fifteen native wildflowers. The pamphlet of the survey explains: "Phenology is the study of the timing of events that happen every year in the lives of plants or animals. . . . This information is used to predict the best time to plant vegetables or crops, in order to get greatest yields and *accurately predict insect outbreaks*" (emphasis added).

That inspired me. What, after all, is a hatch, as fly-fishers think of it, if not an insect outbreak? In his most recent book, *Great Rivers & Great Hatches,* Charles R. Meck, perhaps the dean of angling hatch-chasers, tentatively notes that the blooming of flowers can be a guide to anglers' hatches. But Meck and others cautiously making this connection refer to domestic flowers blooming in the yard at home. That is not good enough simply because the factors and conditions that cause flowers to bloom there can be very different from those out on the stream. At home, the flowers are coddled, cultivated, fertilized; the light intensity is different, and there is radiant heat from building foundations—all factors that artificially affect growth and blooming.

Out on the stream, the most critical factor affecting both the blooming of wildflowers and the hatching of aquatic insects is temperature over the development period. But photoperiod, the relative length of daylight to darkness, also affects the time of blooming in flowers and, some authorities believe, the time of hatching in insects. After some long and patient observation, I came to share the belief that the blooming of certain wildflowers native to my area is an accurate predictor of the timing of certain of my favorite super hatches.

For my home area, Alberta in general, and central Alberta in particular, the photographic combinations of insect and flower in this book are critical. But I emphasize the obvious: the flower-insect combinations that work for my region do not work where the insects exist but the flowers do not. The first Green and Brown Drake hatches I experienced, for example, were on Henry's Fork in Idaho. I do not know whether Wolf Willow or Marsh Marigolds grow along the Fork or, even if they do, whether the Browns hatch to the blooming of the former and the Greens to the latter as they do at home. In fact, my experience on Henry's Fork is that the two big Mayflies often come off on the same days, the Greens in the morning and afternoon and the Browns at dusk. But I have a slide, taken with a telephoto lens to compress the upriver crowds fishing at Last Chance on a day when I caught both hatches, and there are masses of a yellow flower in the foreground. Now that may be a phenological double, and I wish I could tell you what that flower was, but those were the days before I was making my flower-insect connections. I am not alone in making such connections. Recently, I grinned to hear Henry's Fork guru Mike Lawson say he knows the Salmonflies will be emerging on the Warm River-Ashton stretch of the Fork when the Chokecherries are blooming down there.

Much of what I know about insects I have learned away from home, from the streams and their anglers in British

Columbia, Montana, Idaho, Wyoming, Washington. . . . You do not chase hatches long before you learn that the insects that are the essential ingredient of the super hatches are fundamentally the same everywhere in the West.

In fact, there are worldwide similarities. In 1987, in England, I participated in Duffer's Fortnight of the Mayfly hatch, *Ephemera danica,* on the Test. I could not differentiate these Mayflies from our Brown Drake *(Ephemera simulans)* without peering at how the sexual parts fit together like a key into a lock to insure racial purity—"keying," or "peeny popping," as entomologists call it. When the fish got fullish and difficult just as they do during our Brown Drake hatch, the Brit solution was to give them a tiny Blue Dun, just as we sometimes give them a tiny Blue-wing Olive in the North American West.

Invariably, some localized super hatches can occur, as we shall see later, and the timing of the more common hatches can be very different from area to area, depending on climate, altitude and so on. Generally, for example, Alberta's Giant Stonefly hatches are a month earlier than they are on Montana's Madison. But photographs I reviewed recently reminded me that wild roses are in bloom along the Madison when the Golden Stones are hatching there, just as they are along my home waters in Alberta.

For fly-fishers in other parts of the North American West, this book is a guide to a method of meeting and then matching their super hatches. Just as they must always make allowances with hatch tables for local variations in altitude, climate and so forth, they must also make their own flower-insect combinations and connections based on the wild flora of their area.

Some of North America's best trout streams, for example, flow through deserts where the plant life is very different from that of the boreal forest of my west-central Alberta. But most of the super hatch insects in those streams will be the same as, or similar to, those in my home rivers, and plants will be flowering near those desert rivers. The method is the message and vice versa: the super hatch insects will be the same, but fly-fishers need to pick their own flower-indicators. Short-season bloomers are best and most accurate. In my area, for instance, Dogwood blooms all summer, thus telling little about most hatches, except the important Salmonfly hatch taking place when it first starts to bloom.

The phenological connections made at home and practiced during my fishing travels throughout the West over the years have given me more than my fair share of great days fishing super hatches. The text accompanying the photographs in this book offers a brief anecdote from my own experience with each hatch followed by some data about the habits of the insect and its method of emergence. I have included some description of imitations, problems of the hatch and tactics for meeting it that I have learned from the trout and from some very generous tiers and anglers. For fly-fishers in all parts of the West, pains have been taken to show the amateur entomologist in color exactly what each insect looks like. Each is a fresh, live insect. I will not photograph a dead one, except to illustrate the difference in a slide show.

The fishing during a super hatch is generally excellent. It is seldom as easy as it should be, yet it is never as complex as the exact imitation school of fly-tying would have us believe. During thirty years of my own tying I have become more and more a pragmatic impressionist. Some readers will be astonished at the small number of patterns I use. Veteran hatch-chasers will nod wisely. But during a super hatch the trout do become hyperselective, simply because of the sheer numbers of the one insect available to them. The hatch itself programs the trout to eat one thing and one thing only until they are full, and the speed with which that can happen is one real problem of super hatches. But while the steady feeding is happening you generally must have good imitations of the various forms of the natural insect upon which the trout might concentrate.

Because of trout selectivity to "forms" it is important that the fly-fisher understands the terms used to designate the stages of development in the life of Mayflies and Stoneflies, two of the great orders of aquatic insects. *Nymphs* are the underwater forms of both orders. With Stoneflies I simply call the mature, winged form, which hatches from the nymph, the *adult*. The term *emerger* in Mayflies means the nymph in its process of hatching, rising to the surface and splitting open to release the freshly hatched, winged form of the insect, called the *dun*. The *spinner* is the fully mature Mayfly form, after the dun has molted, generally within 24 hours of emergence into the air, following which it mates, deposits its eggs on or in the water and then dies.

The vast majority of fly-fishers I meet do not tie their own flies. They are interested in what works and would just like to be able to buy it. The imitations I suggest in this book, therefore, are usually readily available "off the rack" or are variations of a well-known pattern. For example, the venerable and remarkable Adams in a variety of sizes will match the duns of most of the Mayfly super hatches of western North America.

My advocacy and personal use of the Bastard Adams variation is more for its white wings, which are so much more visible to the angler (and also much easier for the tier) than the traditional grizzly hackle point wings, rather than for any special attraction it holds for the fish. Tying instructions for the Bastard Adams are given in Jack Dennis's *Western Trout Fly Tying Manual,* vol. ii, where credit is given fly-fishing Reverend Dan Abrams. A scant few of the patterns are pure magic in that they seem to solve a problem everyone has with certain hatches. I pass along the credit to each genius who first passed the secret on to me.

Before we get into the acknowledged super hatches and the flowers that signify and predict them for me, let me involve readers in the process. Accompany me on a recent discovery of what *may* be a new Alberta super hatch of an insect not previously known to be common in Alberta but which produces one of the fabled super hatches of eastern North America. Because this hatch is so far confined to one river and has taken place on the same day, four years in a row, it is too soon to call it a super hatch for anyone but me. That very localization and compression, though, provides a short, sharp demonstration of the phenological method of hatch-chasing.

3

YES, ALBERTA, THERE IS A HEX

No matter how large or abundant the aquatic insect, it is not an anglers' super hatch until the trout say so—since 1991 that has been my problem with *Hexagenia limbata*, western North America's largest Mayfly. Though often rumored among anglers, it has never been proven by them to exist in Alberta, despite various entomological assurances, most recently by Dr. Hugh Clifford in *Aquatic Invertebrates of Alberta*. Strangely, many angling entomologists write that the Hex is important in the West but remain vague on exactly where. There are virtually no accounts of fishing western Hex hatches, at least partially because night-fishing is illegal in many places in the West.

Occasionally, Alberta anglers have given me samples of large, "two-tailed" Mayflies, but they invariably turned out to be just Brown Drakes *(Ephemera simulans)* with one of their three tails knocked off. But in midsummer of 1990, several kindly gents gave me a pill bottle of desiccated, huge, golden, two-tailed Mayflies, told me exactly where and when they got them (purely by virtue of staying astream much later than usual) and asked me what they were.

"Hexagenia limbata," I said, in Italica, my voice trembling.

Because these gents speak Latin no more than I, I had to add that this creature triggers the super hatch in the East where it is misnamed the Michigan Caddis, the only logic being that Michigan is where its hatches are alleged to drive huge trout to transports of gluttony on many rivers such as the fabled Au Sable and Pere Marquette.

So, early in July 1992, I dug and strained Alberta mud and marl in the kinds of places the books say Hex nymphs like to dig their U-shaped underwater burrows. I found a few Hex nymphs. Then, on the very day on which the gents said they had caught their adults the year before, just as I was leaving at full dark, a blizzard of Hex duns appeared in my headlights, drifting over the bridge railing, flying upstream. So busy was I catching, bottling and cooling samples that it did not even occur to me to check whether any of the very large Brown trout in this currently unfashionable Alberta trout stream were noticing what I was noticing.

Dr. Clifford at the University of Alberta confirmed my identification, so I became determined to forget collecting and fish the Hex hatch in 1993. That year the dun storm came off on exactly the same late July day as before, but the river oozed pure mud from the coldest July on record and no fish rose. I concentrated on catching perfect specimens, then finding a late Wood (or Tiger) Lily flower-indicator on which to photograph them.

Nineteen ninety-four offered little more hope because early in July we got into the doggiest of Dog Days—hot, bright, humid days with water temperatures of 70 degrees F.—with no hatches of any kind and no rising fish anywhere. I was determined to stay the course. If there really were a major hatch late in July that enticed big trout to feed, that would be important news to fly-fishers in my area.

My task was made easier when the ideal applicant offered to help with my night hatch-watches, an insomnia sufferer to whose repose it makes little difference whether he stays home counting sheep or stays out all night counting aquatic insects—or magically rising trout. I'll call him Insomniac to protect him from inquiries. After all, we had discovered the only place I know where a Hex hatch occurs in the West, and it was handed to me by fly-fishers who didn't even realize what they had. If I or Insomniac breach their trust, who else will ever take us into their confidence?

By 10:15 the same July night as always, nothing had happened. God's dogs had even finished their yipping and howling. Then suddenly a couple of the huge Hex duns lumbered against the last light of the setting sun and Sirius, its dogging Dog Star for which these days are named.

"Set up your rod," I suggested. This should have been done earlier, but hatch-chasers are cynics. What other hatch ever takes place during the Dog Days, let alone on the same day four years in a row? What kind of hatch table has only one date?

"They're drifting over the bridge by the hundreds," I said before Insomniac could get his rod strung.

By then the many wings were rustling like soft wind or rain in Aspen leaves, but we could also hear, amplified by the muggy night and the sound chamber under the bridge, the glops, gunks and gushes of big fish suddenly feeding in the dark of the river below.

Because I needed more photos for this book, I stayed on

the bridge with an insect net while Insomniac slid down the
bank with one of my extended-body, parachute-style Hex dun
imitations imported straight from Michigan for the occasion.
(Since then I have found Kaufmanns in Portland to be a sup-
plier of reliable Hex imitations.)

"Fish on!" Insomniac announced as I was putting the last
sample bottle in the cooler.

Only then did we discover that my night fishing lights were
in my garage back in the city.

In the dark Insomniac landed a Brown trout of about eighteen inches while I wrestled with my infrared beam, auto-focus-
in-the-dark camera that just would not fire on this historic
night.

"Got another one," I heard as I arrived back at the rig for
another camera and an ordinary flashlight. This second Brown
was considerably longer than twenty inches with a sickle hook
on his lower jaw counterpointing and reflecting light from the
waning, sickle moon that was just rising. Maybe we even got a
picture. Whether it was the moonlight, the flashlight or the
camera flash, the rises stopped. It was nearly midnight.

Insomniac was utterly content. Maybe fly-fisher's heaven is
to discover a super hatch in the darkest Dog Days and be one
of maybe half a dozen people in the world who knows about
it. He even offered to climb through the fence on a lease road
into an oil well site to pluck me a few blooms from a clump of
Gaillardia (Brown-eyed Susan) I remembered seeing there.
Over the three years that I have caught this hatch on the same
day each year, I have become dissatisfied with the late-bloom-
ing Wood Lily I found on that first night and now rely on
Gaillardia to remind me when it is Hex time on the little river.

A rig turned in behind us. Probably the oil company or the farmer, I thought, checking for rustlers of Alberta crude . . . or cows. I drove up to where I could give him room to turn around. From there, in the headlights of the other truck, I saw someone helping Insomniac and his fistful of gold and burgundy posies through the fence.

"I told him I was with this maniac who likes to photograph rare insects on wildflowers in the middle of the night," Insomniac said when we were safely back on the road and on our way.

"What'd he say?" I asked.

"Just don't be too long about it."

Hexagenia limbata on Gaillardia (Gaillardia aristata)

4

WESTERN MARCH BROWN

Rithrogena species

O N A BLACK DAY in mid-May of an awful spring fifteen years ago, my doctor, Jake Reimer, called and we went fishing. To Jake's occasional days off and unseasonal urges to fish I owe the discovery that many super hatches take place during wet, cold, even stormy weather when few anglers fish.

As I stood in the riffle at the head of a big pool soaking a lead-weighted streamer, I swore I could see rises in an eddy down below but could see no insect anywhere. Eventually, I went down, put nose to water and looked back up against the light. There, sailing serenely, were hundreds of nearly black, #14 Mayfly duns almost invisible on the steel gray waters reflecting the dark spring skies.

That early in the season I did not expect rising fish and had not bothered to bring the dry-fly boxes. But two or three of last season's #10 Le Tort Hoppers were left on the patch of my vest, each with a white deer-hair wing. In desperation I tried one, and several good Browns took the ludicrous, inexact imitation, the trout as demented by a hatch after a long Alberta winter as the cabin-fevered angler.

Since then, on many Alberta, Montana and British Columbia rivers and streams, I have caught the hatch of these early spring Mayflies. In 1989 I put it all together—my soup strainer, collecting bottles and macrophotography equipment. I even found an emerging wild Clematis on which to pose my specimens of the Western March Brown and now find the blooming of this flower a reliable predictor of my March Brown hatches.

Western March Brown on Clematis (Clematis verticellaris)

EMERGENCE DATA

The nymph is a clinger, a creature of fast water and rocky bottoms that emerges in quiet eddies beside fast water, particularly after noon on blustery, gray spring days. In my area it emerges in late April and early May. In more gentle climates, on the coast, for example, it emerges in March.

IMITATIONS

The dun has two tails, a dark olive body and an almost black, heavily veined wing. My best imitation is a #12 or #14 Adams, particularly the Bastard Adams with the white calf-tail wing or with the white polypropylene yarn that I prefer in my version.

Bastard Adams

PROBLEMS AND TACTICS

Once you see these big, dark flies, you may overlook the season's first tiny Blue-winged Olives *(Baetis)* hatching among them. But the trout notice and sometimes prefer the smaller fly. If the fish keep rising but ignore your #12s and #14s, switch to a #16 or #18 Blue-winged Olive pattern or even a Bastard Adams in the same smaller size.

5

BLUE-WINGED OLIVE

Baetis species

IT WAS my last evening of three September days I had been
fishing the lower Bow River with two innovative angling
legends, Lefty Kreh of Baltimore, Maryland, and the late
Charlie Brooks of West Yellowstone, Montana. Lefty had
departed for home after giving me more tips, hints and help
than I could ever thank him for, except by divulging my secret
for landing big trout despite the Bow's heavy weed—a #16
hook with an eye big enough to take a 2x leader. We had both
been wincing all afternoon as Charlie kept popping 5x tippets
and feeding big Bow River trout Grey Fox Variants tied by
Art Flick himself.

An Adams, actually a #16 tied on a #14 hook, was what I
selected that frosty, drizzly evening when a good hatch of
Blue-winged Olives came on, inspiring a rise of big trout in
chest-deep water on the far side of a floating weed bank.
Charlie, tired from a long day and the effects of his recent
bypass surgery, decided to stay in the drift boat and exercise
his new camera.

I was using a new nine-foot Orvis rod that was just long
enough to reach over the weeds, so I could dap and get a drag-

free float over the risers. Starting with the farthest down-stream, every fish in the pod took, and that 2x leader held often enough to haul most of them through the weeds.

When it was too dark and cold to continue, Charlie helped me back into the boat. "Not bad, kid," he said. "Seven hooked, five landed and not one under twenty inches."

Blue-winged Olive on Poplar bud (Populus tremuloides)

EMERGENCE DATA

The nymph is a swimmer of moderate flows over varied bottom types. It is said to have two generations per year, but experienced hatch-watchers expect to see *Baetis* duns any time from the first of March to the middle of November and even on nice January and February days on spring creeks that stay open all winter, such as Alberta's North Raven or the many fine spring creeks in Montana and Idaho. Blue-winged Olives frequently start hatching about noon on dark, damp, even stormy days. Although there are often late fall wildflowers around when the fall *Baetis* hatches start, somehow I always associate this hatch, spring or fall, with Aspen leaf buds, dormant or just starting to burst.

IMITATIONS

Rarely are these flies as large as #14. They range mostly from #16s to #18s down to "no-seeums." In my part of the country, the Blue-winged Olives seem to get smaller as the season grows later. The dun has two tails. The wing is a smoky

Bastard Adams

blue to black, and the body is olive, often very dark. The large orange eyes are visible on even the smallest specimens. There are many good Blue-winged Olive dun patterns. The preference of my weak-eyed self and my wing-blind quarry is the Bastard Adams, again, in sizes from #14 down to #18 and smaller.

PROBLEMS AND TACTICS

Because the Blue-winged Olive emerges any time of the year, the fly-fisher must be ever watchful. Often its emergence is lost among many larger, seemingly more succulent morsels. However, trout often prefer the smaller insect. The most extreme example I recall was the day angling artist Jack Cowin, using #6 Salmonfly imitations, simply could not catch a trout rising constantly by a beaver house during a Salmonfly hatch. I had been noticing some tiny, emerging Blue-winged Olives, suggested he switch to #16 Adams, and he took the fish with the first cast. Later, he memorialized the event with one of his limited-edition etchings.

6

GIANT STONES
Salmonfly and Golden Stone

Pteronarcys californica, **and** *Acroneuria*
calineuria **and** *Hesperoperla* **species**

THE FISHING suddenly looked up when I did, one cold, drizzly Canada Day (July 1st) several years ago down on the Crowsnest River before it became famous even in Alberta.

Before heading back empty-handed to the bridge game at the ranch, I looked up to see a sight I recognized from Montana and Idaho. Thousands of creatures—like slow hummingbirds—were milling at treetop level, dipping ever nearer the water. Soon the big adult Stoneflies—mixed Salmonflies and Golden Stones—began crash-diving into the water, then flying upstream to let the surface tension pull the eggs from their abdomens.

The fluttering on the surface attracted fish, and the flies began disappearing in bursts of spray. I had none of the larger salmon-colored imitations, only #8 Yellow-bodied Le Tort Hoppers. On this occasion the difference did not seem to matter.

Every time I got to the top end of a long cutbank, I just walked back down and fished up again. I lost count how many really large Rainbows I caught that day before I quit when my hands no longer worked and I was near hypothermia. But I had been to heaven and back: a major egg-laying run, a brush hatch of our two largest Stoneflies on the Canadian national holiday with not another angler in sight.

Salmonfly on Dogwood (Cornus stolonifera)

Golden Stone on wild rose (Rosa acicularis)

EMERGENCE DATA

Although the Salmonfly emergence generally precedes the Golden Stone's by about a week or two, they often appear simultaneously as early as mid-May in some central Alberta streams, such as the South Raven, or as late as the end of July for the Golden Stone on the North Ram. The difference is altitude and temperature. The North Ram is higher, its waters always colder than the central Alberta Brown trout streams. The nymph of both species inhabits fast, cool, boulder-strewn and well-oxygenated sections of rivers and streams. The Salmonfly nymph is dark brown or black; the Golden Stone is grayish and handsomely marked.

The hatch is long if you count the migration of the nymph from the water to emerge as an adult on rocks and streamside foliage, and then add the brush hatch when the winged adult finally mates and returns to the water to lay its eggs. I always associate the emergence of the Salmonfly nymph with the first Dogwood buds in my area. But in some years, by the time the Salmonfly adult gets around to its egg-laying brush hatch, the wild roses are in bloom and the Golden Stone, which gets to the facts of life more quickly, is also down on the water, laying eggs and driving fish and fly-fishers mad.

The nymphs of both species have at least a two- and possibly a four-year underwater life-span before they emerge as adults. Thus, immature nymphs of varying sizes of these species are always in the water, making them the largest and most important item in the diets of trout in the streams in which they occur.

IMITATIONS

For the Golden Stone nymph, weighted Gold-ribbed Hare's Ear nymphs in sizes #6 to #10 are generally all you need. (My version employs copper wire and Red Squirrel fur.) For the egg-laying adults during the brush hatches, I have always used Yellow-bodied Le Tort Hoppers, in sizes #6 to #10, clipped out carefully on the underside so the bodies ride in the surface film, showing their color to the trout. In recent years I have used Stimulators, particularly to fish them downstream and across, making them drag against the current, skitter and flutter like the naturals are doing in the wind.

Gold-ribbed Hare's Ear

Yellow-bodied Le Tort Hopper

Somehow the Salmonfly is more complex. People swear by black nymphs like the Montana Stone or the Brooks' Stone, but I have always done better with the brown Bird's Stonefly. The

Bird's Stonefly nymph

Salmonfly nymph sheds its skin many times during its long underwater life, and, between stages or instars, it is soft, succulent and brown. The fish seem to relish it.

For the adult, I generally use the Le Tort Hopper, again, this time in sizes #4 to #8, with a pink polypropylene body. Occasionally, particularly when it is windy, the fish seem to favor a fluttery presentation of a double-hackled Sofa Pillow or an orange-bodied Stimulator. My personal favorite is a heavily hackled fly with deer-hair wings tied on a reversed #6 hook. The fly seems to skitter well and shows the pink loop at the end of the body, representing the egg mass, particularly well to the trout.

Brown Salmonfly nymph

Black Salmonfly nymph

PROBLEMS AND TACTICS

The emergence of the Salmonfly and Golden Stone nymph is easy to locate for any observant angler with lots of time and a little knowledge of when it happens on his section of stream. On my favorite Stonefly water I watch for Dogwood flower buds to signal the Salmonfly and wild rose blooms to signal the Golden Stone.

Reversed-hook Skittering Salmonfly

But predicting when the mated Salmonfly female will return from the trees to the water to lay its eggs is the most frustrating endeavor in hatch-chasing. Salmonfly brush hatches are unpredictable because they often occur at night and because the creature can feed as an adult and thus is in no hurry to mate and die. As already noted, the Golden Stone seems to mate and lay its eggs much sooner after emergence. The Golden also seems to emerge over a longer period of time on a given stretch of stream than does the Salmonfly, which is famous for being an upstream-progressive hatch.

Pink-bodied Le Tort Hopper

Golden Stone nymph

If adults of both species are present, the trout often prefer the smaller Golden Stone and key on the color of the body being dipped in the water. Switching to a smaller Yellow-bodied Le Tort Hopper, #8 or #10, generally solves the problem, as it did for me, my son and nephew on America's national holiday several years ago on a side-channel of the lower Madison River, perhaps North America's most perfect Giant Stonefly habitat.

It is never a mistake to fish weighted Giant Stone nymph imitations in the rivers and streams inhabited by naturals when there is no obvious surface activity of insects or fish.

7

WESTERN GREEN DRAKE

Ephemerella or *Drunella,*
mostly *grandis,* species

IT WAS A BIZARRE initiation to one of fly-fishing's world-class events: the Green Drake hatch on Idaho's Henry's Fork of the Snake River early in July. Friend Lloyd Graff and I were rigging up on a service road beside the Fork near Last Chance. Suddenly, profanity broke out, something so common on the frustrating Fork that I did not look up until it became sulphuric. Against the sky, hanging over the sagebrush on the far side, a hot orange fly line draped from a sea gull, which the fisherman was obliged to play like a kite. Sea gulls love the huge, fat Mayflies and will take a good, dry-dun imitation faster even than big Rocky Mountain Whitefish can gum one and slime good hackle into spitballs. The trout become paranoid about the competition, some rejecting dry-dun imitations entirely in favor of feeding underwater on the emerging nymph. Most fly-fishers do not seem to get the message to change to nymphs soon enough.

Lloyd and I shared the misery. We did not hook a sea gull, but their close inspection of our dun imitations was clearly repelling trout. We added our unsophisticated efforts to the profanity that could be heard in many of the world's languages. Eventually, Lloyd fell in, started to shiver and had to retreat to our car and its heater. I just let my line trail far downstream as I attempted to photograph the gulls mugging the flies of my nearest enraged neighbor. My biggest trout of the day—wise, sophisticated, striking on that sunken, dragging fly—nearly dislocated my shoulder and did break my leader. We adjourned to lunch and to digest whatever our first great Green Drake hatch had taught us and plot to redeem ourselves with the Brown Drakes that evening.

Green Drake on Marsh Marigold (Caltha palustris L.)

EMERGENCE DATA

The nymph of the Western Green Drake, the third largest of the West's Mayflies, is a crawler that inhabits smooth water of moderate flow in big rivers or small streams with bottoms of small to medium gravel. In Alberta we find it hatching in times and places as varied as June on the tiny North Raven, July on the Crowsnest and late July and into mid-August on the higher, colder North Ram. My flower association for the Green Drake is always the Marsh Marigold that lines the North Raven when the Green Drake is hatching there. Everywhere I have fished it, emergence has generally started about 10:00 A.M. for this lover of gloomy, drizzly days.

The standing dun can be an inch vertically from wingtip to tiptoes. It has three tails and a smoky, bluish gray wing. When first hatched, its fat body is as plump, juicy and green as a lime. But the color quickly changes to mahogany. The large red eyes are a startling feature.

IMITATIONS

Generally, a weighted Gold-ribbed Hare's Ear, #10 or #12, will do as the nymph imitation while an unweighted version works for the emerging nymph that has just arrived at the surface. Many excellent commercial ties are available for the

Gold-ribbed Hare's Ear

dun, two of the best being a greenish Wulff-style and an

extended-body parachute-style. I use a #10 Hair-wing Variant in preference to even the Bastard Adams and sometimes foolishly speculate that the striping of the Variant's quill body may make a difference, even though its over-sized hackle holds the body well off the water where the trout probably cannot see its detail.

PROBLEMS AND TACTICS

The largest Rainbow I have taken on a fly—twenty-eight inches—was blissfully taking only the very occasional Green Drake coming along during a heavy Pale Morning Dun hatch in a section of the Crowsnest where popular wisdom holds that there are only small fish. Obviously, this fish was still keying on the larger, more succulent stragglers of the hatch that was coming to its seasonal end in preference to the vastly more abundant—but smaller—insects of the hatch that was just coming into season.

Sometimes the angler has to experiment to find what form of the insect the fish are taking—nymph, emerger or dun—and Western Green Drakes are no exception.

Where Western Green Drake waters are smooth and placid, like those of the Fork, a downstream, slack-line cast, causing the fish to see the fly before leader, often solves a multitude of problems, except the sea gulls. For them, I suggest a riot gun and #7 ½ shot.

8

BROWN DRAKE

Ephemera simulans

BEFORE HE DIED in November 1993, my fishing buddy Lloyd Graff frequently commented that we just were not getting enough Brown Drake evenings. He was right.

Lloyd loved Brown Drake hatches above all others, particularly when they started about 8:30 on a beautiful Wolf Willow-scented evening and went on until dark. He did not keep a fishing diary and always insisted that such evenings took place in July. He was always outraged when I phoned him in June to tell him the Browns were hatching.

But for at least the previous three years, the West's second-largest Mayfly has been hatching on dark, cool and drizzly days, starting even in the morning, just before the annual June monsoon in our part of the country.

Last year the rains came somewhat earlier and the Brown Drakes did not hatch during the storms. Then the hatch seemed to be delayed by the resulting high, cold and muddy water.

But, just in case, I kept under surveillance my favorite slow-flowing, mud- and marl-bottomed piece of perfect habitat for the burrowing nymphs of the Brown Drake. One afternoon it looked as though the water was down somewhat and there was enough visibility for a trout to see a big Mayfly hatching in big numbers.

Sure enough, at 8:30 that mid-June evening, a few freshly hatched big duns sailed down along the far bank to where three fish were eating them. It figured—just an evening when Barbara, my wife, and Red, our Brittany, had to leave for home at nine.

There was just time to tie on a #10 Bastard Adams, my favorite Brown Drake dun imitation, pick out what looked like the largest fish, then hook, horse in and release a male Brown trout that was at least twenty-four inches long.

But next evening I was on deck in plenty of time, prepared to stay up all night if necessary. When I arrived, a few fully molted Brown drake spinners were already doing their rising-falling mating dance above a riffle. Two big trout in a backwater were quietly sipping spent spinners that had deposited their eggs and expired.

One of these trout took my extended-body parachute-style dun imitation when I was not looking, and I struck the sound. The fish, probably foul-hooked, took the entire fly-line twice and wallowed a lot, its tail like a grub hoe waving in the air. Eventually, I got impatient, palmed the reel too hard and the 2x leader snapped like a shot.

The next fish announced itself like a flushing toilet as I tied on a new tippet. The duns were now hatching and getting off the water instantly because the evening was so warm and dry. This big fish was fielding them left, right and center, like a shortstop, making an awesome commotion in the shallow water in the tail of the pool just upstream.

He ate my fly as soon as he saw it, too, but it came loose

quickly. Those big, extended-body parachute ties seem to do that a lot.

Then, in a little bay in the bank upstream, I spotted the quiet rises of an old master—neb, dorsal, tail wiggle, bubble. This one, I decided, must be taking the spent and dying spinners that he knows cannot fly away.

But he would not take my flat-out spent-spinner imitation, nor would he look at the extended-body parachute. Though he took the first Bastard Adams I showed him, it, too, did not stick.

Amend that. Big Mayfly imitations of any kind just do not stick well. I hooked seven fish but landed only two, both over twenty inches, before the full moon rose and everything stopped —bugs, fish and me.

The next evening Jim Wiseman called to see if I could come out to play and guide with him and Robert Short. My wife said okay as long as someone else was driving, it being her opinion that these constant night-hatch stakeouts were too much for an old guy.

Little was happening when we arrived, except a few spinners doing their swooping mating dance above every riffle. Robert missed hooking a large trout to a small, quiet rise to his fly in a backwater where I had lost the big one the night before. Jim got out his big nymph seine and posthole digger and started seining mud for nymphs. Not a one did he find—a bad sign that the hatch might be over for the year.

Then big flies started cruising the surface, fish started eating them, the gents started fishing and I started catching and photographing insects. But they were all molted, half-spent, egg-laying spinners—not a freshly hatched dun among them. Perhaps this would be the hatch's last evening.

Meanwhile, fly-fishers and fish were enjoying it while it lasted. Brown Drake hooking percentages held: half to two-thirds of the time the hook came loose. Occasionally, a leader snapped on the strike. But there were some good pictures of my human models releasing very large models piscatorial.

Then, suddenly, with the rising moon just an orange glow in the east, it was over. There was time to smell the flowers of the Wolf Willow and have a beer.

We drank a toast to our mutual, departed friend, Lloyd Graff, who had fished this pool dozens of times.

Did I just imagine his chuckle and voice? "It just doesn't get any better than this. Anywhere."

Brown Drake on Wolf Willow (Elaeagnus commutata)

Brown Drake on Heart-leaved Arnica (Arnica cordifolia)

EMERGENCE DATA

The Brown Drake nymph of the West's second largest Mayfly (the standing dun is more than an inch high and long) is a burrower that inhabits U-shaped tunnels about five inches deep in the silt, sand, or marl bottoms of some slow, smooth trout streams. Alberta's Raven River system has heavy hatches, particularly the North Raven in early June. I have also fished excellent hatches early in July on Henry's Fork and the upper Gibbon River in Yellowstone Park.

Each year, for a week or so in early July, the mature nymph exits its burrow permanently, and the dun pops to the surface and rides it for twenty feet or so before its wings are dry and it can fly, giving the fish ample opportunity to take a good mouthful of protein. The gorgeous dun has three tails; its body is cream on the underside and has a cream and brown diamond pattern on top. The wing is clear brown and heavily marked with a nearly black pattern.

IMITATIONS

Complex, hard-to-tie commercial nymph patterns are available, but a roughly tied, lightly weighted Gold-ribbed Hare's Ear will serve as both the nymph and emerger patterns.

Gold-ribbed Hare's Ear

The imitation dun should be tied on light wire #10 2x- or 3x-long hooks. As with the Green Drake, commercial Wulff-style and extended-body parachute-style imitations work well, both of which I once used exclusively. But one night I was surprised to spy in the gloom my young friend Ron Dutcher using nothing but—what else?—something he called the Bastard Adams. He said he could see it more easily in Brown Drake light conditions.

Late in a hatch the trout can become selective about the spent spinners. In such situations, a #10 pattern with a brown and cream body and spent, brown-dyed grizzly hackle wings can do brisk business.

PROBLEMS AND TACTICS

As with the Western Green Drake, the most prevalent Brown Drake problem is what form of the insect a particular fish is taking. But with the Brown it can be the complete menu of forms: nymph, emerger, dun or spinner. On some nights the fish seem to prefer an extended-body, parachute dry-dun imitation over a traditional tie; on other evenings they prefer the opposite. If a fish is keying on the emerging nymph, a deadly tactic is to get upstream, let your nymph swing across and up just in front of the trout's position and then prepare for a heavy strike. Jim Wiseman does well during Brown Drake hatches fishing two flies: the nymph-emerger under a dry-dun imitation.

There are other practical problems with this hatch. In the tiny North Raven it is always difficult to land the large Brown trout hooked during the hatch. The last time I fished the hatch on Henry's Fork, the catch was ten to a dozen Whitefish for every Rainbow, and I began to appreciate the fabled one hundred per day Whitefish holocaust on the Fork.

9

PALE MORNING DUN

Ephemerella inermis
and *infrequens*

O N YET ANOTHER drizzly, blustery mid-June afternoon I
arrived at a favorite spot I call the Drive-in Theater
because I have standing permission to drive right into a park-
ing spot by the stream and there is often something sexy going
on when I get there.

This time, at 4:00 P.M., under darkening skies threatening
serious rain, I happened upon one of the heaviest hatches of
Pale Morning Duns I have ever seen. The event was made
especially unusual by its timing: early in the month and late in
the day. The long, smooth run of tiny, pale yellow duns was a
gold carpet from bank to bank.

Fifteen large trout had been lured from under the cutbank
and brush piles by the insect hordes, and they were rising
steadily, even in very shallow water on the near side. My Pale
Morning Dun imitations were on back order, but I did have
three of Lloyd Graff's exquisite #18 Bastard Adams. By the
time driving rain stopped the hatch at 6:00 P.M., I had three
Browns—measuring fourteen, eighteen and twenty inches—
and had lost two of my precious flies to bigger fish.

The last half hour I spent trying to catch the Shark, the

largest fish in the run, patrolling the head of it in regal majesty, slashing right and left with his dorsal fin and the top lobe of its tail out of the water. He was not taking either floating natural duns or my imitation, though the bulge of his rise was often so close that my fly surfed right over his furrowed forehead. He would not take nymphs either. The driving rain saved me from having to admit I had just given up.

Pale Morning Dun on Canada Anenome (Anemone canadensis L.)

Pale Morning Dun on Bunchberry (Cornus canadensis L.)

EMERGENCE DATA

Many fly-fishers contend that the Pale Morning Dun is the North American West's most important super hatch. Certainly, it is one of our more reliable, widespread and longer hatches. *Ephemerella inermis* and *infrequens* are the principal cause of the exceptional dry fly-fishing that has made the lower Bow famous. Because this hatch takes place for a month or two in most places, many flowers could serve as stages for my pictures. My favorites are either the Canada Anemone or the Canada Flower, the Bunchberry, both in bloom throughout the hatch.

The nymphs of the two species, together called PMDs, are crawlers and prefer to emerge on the flatter, smoother stretches of even the roughest streams in which they live. The dun ranges in size from #14 down to #20, has three tails and looks pale yellow on the water. The body is actually light olive and the wings are smoky blue. These creatures love cool, breezy, overcast days and float, twitching, a long time before their wing muscles warm up enough for flight. Frequently, the wind capsizes the duns. Trout—BIG trout—love them.

IMITATIONS

No Mayfly super hatch inspires a greater variety of ingenious, innovative dun patterns than does the PMD hatch. This is a reflection not only of the importance of the hatch but also of its frustrations: every serious fly-fisher tells tales of days when nothing would work while the trout were obviously gorging during a heavy PMD hatch.

But many grizzled veterans still swear by the the traditional Light Cahill or Ginger Quill patterns. My favorites are a hen-wing thorax tie and a tan elk-hair-winged no-hackle, especially for the smooth waters. For the rougher waters, I prefer the Bastard Adams with good grizzly and brown hackle mixed on #16 to #20 hooks.

Bastard Adams

PROBLEMS AND TACTICS

This hatch has many problems in addition to the practical one posed by the sheer number of naturals competing for the fishes' attention on the water and the philosophical one arising from whether the fish are taking nymphs, emergers or duns, or whether the spent spinners interest them at all. Anyone who has fished many Pale Morning Dun hatches will carry swarms of new and different imitations. They will change flies feverishly to cover those situations when the fish are rising regularly but do not seem to be taking floating duns and will not look at anything artificial, even nymphs. It is frustrating to watch every floating thing just slide over the leading bulge of their last rise.

In the past few seasons a remarkable solution to these problems for me has been the Pale Morning Dun Emerger in sizes #16 and #18 that I first obtained from Craig Mathews of Blue Ribbon Flies in West Yellowstone. Now I can tie my own at the rate of one every two minutes. My version is obviously

completely patterned on Blue
Ribbon's. It has brown zelon in
the tail position to represent the
trailing nymphal shuck, pale
poly yellow yarn for the body,
grizzly or blue dun hackle
trimmed top and bottom, and a
bulging strip of gray polycelon

Pale Morning Dun emerger

foam over the top of the hackle to represent the wings just
emerging from the nymphal shuck. I fish this one untreated,
floating awash in the surface film.

Stubborn fish that are obviously feeding on the millions of
duns can frequently be attracted with a downstream cast and
the application of just a little drag—on purpose and at the
right time to make your fly stand out from the rest.

10

Trico

Tricorythodes species

D E MINIMUS NON CURAT LEX: The law, as all we lawyers know, takes no notice of trifles. But fish do, and thus fly-fishers should love the Trico, our smallest Mayfly. Its mating spinners form blizzards over the riffles and gravel bars of virtually every trout stream in the West every mid-morning from mid-August to mid-October and even to freeze-up in some places. When I start noticing blue wildflowers again—Harebells, Asters—after the reds and yellows of summer, I start looking for Tricos.

Most fly-fishers are cleaned out and burnt out by fishing tiny imitations of the balling, falling, egg-laying spinners. Lloyd Graff and I wondered when all those duns hatched to molt and form those accursed mid-morning spinners. That is why we arrived at 8:00 A.M. one cool, damp and gray September morning at a long, deep pool on a central Alberta creek. We were pleasantly surprised to see the surface already sparkling with the million points of light reflecting from the wings of millions of tiny Trico duns.

We tied on #20 and #22 dun imitations to 5x leaders—flies that had been given to me in Idaho on Henry's Fork the previous season by Dave Engerbretson. But since then, the tiny hooks had become corroded from too many soakings from my too-frequent deep wading. The big Browns came more faithfully to these dun imitations than they ever did to spinner imitations. My first fish surged upstream and around the bend to the right, and then everything went slack. The tiny hook had broken at its bend. Over and over the same thing happened to both of us until we had fed all those flawed flies to the big Browns. Down the trail we went, babbling. We had proved that Trico duns emerge early in the morning and had a successful early morning fishing to them—without landing fish number one!

Trico on Bluebell (Harebell) (Campanula rotundifolia L.)

EMERGENCE DATA

The Trico nymph, our tiniest Mayfly, is a crawler that prefers small rubble bottoms of rivers and streams of medium flow. The hatch seems to take place in the cool of the early morning. Then the dun molts, swarms and mates later the same morning when the air reaches the appropriate temperature. Back channels of islands in the Bow provide great Trico fishing, just as they do on Henry's Fork and the Madison on mornings from late July to late October. The dun has three tails, a black body and an almost clear, single wing. The spinner is similar but has a clear wing. Sizes range from invisible up to, rarely, as large as #18.

IMITATIONS

Obtaining good imitations is a problem simply because few amateurs can tie this small. Hell, I have to take a brain surgeon along just to tie mine on the leader!

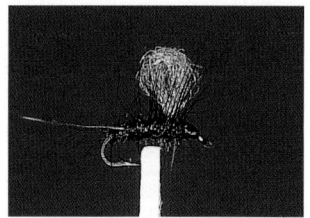

Loop-wing Trico dun

A variety of commercial imitations is available, generally black-bodied with white poly yarn wings. Every fly box should have a few of both the spent-wing spinner imitations and the up-wing or loop-wing dun.

I buy my Trico imitations locally from the best fly-fishing stores or order from the likes of Dan Bailey's in Livingston, Montana, or Blue Ribbon in West Yellowstone.

PROBLEMS AND TACTICS

If the water is a little rough and bumpy, locating rises of even the biggest fish that relish these tiny morsels can be difficult. Listen for the curious tap-tapping sound that many good Trico fly-fishers on the Bow have noted. They speculate it is the sound of the roof of the mouth slapping the water as the fish eat Tricos by the mouthful. On lakes such as Hebgen in Montana, Trico-eating fish are called Gulpers for the sound they make as they cruise along, browsing on Tricos.

As with any fly that hatches in the millions and that the fish love, another problem is having a particular fish include your imitation in one of the mouthfuls of naturals he is gulping. Some brain surgeons tie on two or three imitations, clumped, with the one knot at the leader point. Others will tie two and even three imitations on one #16 long-shank, light-wire hook.

One magic solution I first learned from Leigh Perkins, then president of Orvis, when we were fishing in central Alberta, was the use of a #18 or #20 Flying Red Ant pattern during a difficult Trico hatch—and I mean screaming, scarlet red. As

Flying Red Ant

Jim McLennan, author of *The Blue Ribbon Bow,* says: "When it works, it really works; otherwise, not at all." Nobody knows why the Flying Red Ant works when it does, but it is always worth a try.

II

SUPER HATCHES
IN THE FUTURE

Wвариант HAT GENERALLY gets me out too early each year is the hope of finding an earlier super hatch than even Blue-winged Olives or March Browns that will start the trout looking upwards and rising for the new season. For years I have been interested in the tiny, early Stoneflies, collectively called Snowflies, and the considerably larger Early Brown Stones. But the fish never seem interested in the former, and I have never been able to find the latter in much abundance.

Far too early in my most recent season I was dozing in the weak spring sunshine on the bank of the Drive-in Theater when a plop brought me bolt upright in time to see fading ripples near the head of the run. I discounted them as merely the result of a chunk of rotten bank ice breaking off. But when the noise came again, without the ice, I looked up and noticed the flies.

From the spruce tops, medium-sized Stoneflies, about size #12, I decided, were diving straight onto the center of the run, then scurrying for either shore on the surface of the water. Those that went for the far, deep side of the stream were being chased by trout and taken in showy rises.

Early Brown Stone on male Aspen flower (Populus tremuloides)

I selected a #12 green-bodied Stimulator, which is as good a generic, moving Stonefly imitation as there is. It was accepted by the trout instantly, and I took half a dozen Browns up to sixteen inches by the time I got to the head of the run and the fish that had awakened me.

He, too, took instantly and came into my hand in less than a minute, so nearly comatose was he in the frigid water. He had to be my old adversary of Pale Morning Dun hatches, the Shark. Even though I had never hooked him before, I had seen before the grimace the kype on his lower jaw gave him as he ate something in clear water at the head of this run. I had estimated his length at what it was, slightly better than twenty-four inches. This is a remarkable fish for me any time, let alone for an extra early start to a new season.

I have tentatively identified these small, early Stonefly adults as a species of *Brachyptera* though I await confirmation from my Stonefly experts. Whether I have found a locally important super hatch depends on whether it regularly produces so early in the season the kind of dry fly-fishing I experienced that one day. I went looking hard for a flower to serve as a reminder of the hatch for next year and found an early Aspen in full bloom. In early Aspen time next year, I will be out doing further research.

Then there is the other end, the sad end of the season. How late can we extend the good dry fly-fishing, and is there a super hatch in September . . . October?

Late in the summer, back in the good old days when you encountered only bait-fishing locals on the Crowsnest River, I became intrigued by the fat, grinding bellies and distended vents of the trout I was releasing. It was as though they suffered from hemorrhoids. Eventually, I just had to kill and dissect a Rainbow, and a local in the uniform—ball hat, hip waders, industrial-sized creel—caught me at it. I showed him the many sand- and stone-caddis cases, each more than an inch long, that I had taken from the trout's stomach.

"When do these hatch?" I asked.

"What the Hell are those?" he replied, squinting slyly through the smoke of the cigarette glued to his lower lip. I have since learned there are only two kinds of local Crowsnest regular: those who really know nothing about their river and those who lie a lot. I have seen dozens of Crowsnest locals seining live bait, including whatever these creatures were.

Later that season I noticed hundreds of the stone cases anchored on rocks in the shallows. I broke a few open and noted the succulence (to fish, at least) of the long, fat, pale orange Caddis larva inside. The first time I read Gary LaFontaine's monumental work *Caddisflies,* I was struck by his enthusiasm for the *Dicosmoecus* species he calls the Giant Orange Sedge. In his opinion it is the brood mother of all super hatches because it provides North America's best opportunity to catch really large fish.

The Giant Orange Sedge, contends LaFontaine, is the clear winner among super hatches, east and west, for several reasons. Unlike the Eastern Hex, it emerges in daylight when anglers can see it and fish it, and unlike the Western Salmonfly, which so often emerges in late spring when waters are high, dirty and unfishable, it comes on in the fall when the waters run low and clear. As the clincher, he asserts that this huge Caddis inhabits rivers with much larger fish in them than those of the other two super hatches. LaFontaine's praise echoes the enthusiasm of Dave Hughes, in his *Western Stream-side Guide,* for fishing what he calls the Fall Caddis on Oregon's Deschutes. On Alberta's Crowsnest, this creature is called the October Caddis.

Fall Caddis with autumn leaves

In this book I have tried to use minimal Latin and Greek. But the varying common names given to *Dicosmoecus* in various places in North America illustrates that some Latin and Greek is essential so all we plain-talking anglers will know we are referring to the same creature.

LaFontaine says the *Dicosmoecus* is most abundant in California, Washington, Oregon, Alaska and British Columbia, and notes that it is also found in Idaho, Montana and Utah. He says it is also important in west-slope streams in Montana, such as Rock Creek, but notes his difficulties in finding out just when the good fishing to this hatch takes place. East-slope rivers in Montana have only sparse populations, he notes, but a big Orange Sedge pattern is a good searching pattern.

Well, the Crowsnest is an east-slope river. So far it is the only Alberta river in which I have found a large population of *Dicosmoecus*. Trying to net samples of the adult in flight was like trying to catch the world's best knuckle ball. Never have I seen a fish take an October Caddis, but I have seen the odd one swing at and miss the big, dipsy-doodling bundle of protein.

Because of the Fall Caddis adults' large size (#6 or #8) and its orange body, I have even heard anglers along the Crowsnest erroneously identify it as a late Salmonfly—as graphic an illustration as there is of the difficulty anglers have recalling when important hatches take place. Their difficulty, like mine, I suspect, is similar to the one everyone has with the Salmonfly: we have just never been on the Crowsnest when the Fall Caddis adults seriously get down on the water in large numbers to lay their eggs.

The intriguing problem with all hatch-chasing is that none of us lives "wild" any more so that we can haunt even a small stretch of a good stream all the time and thereby always know what is going on in even that small part of the natural world. The hardest thing for even knowledgeable hatch-chasers to accept is that amazing, unseen things may be going on in favorite places, and that the insects do not give a damn for human affairs—not work and vacation schedules, not hatch tables, and certainly not hotlines and computer programs.

This fall, I am planning an extended trip to the Crowsnest, solely for the purpose of seeing if the trout will tell me we have another super hatch. Then and only then will I employ the diabolical methods a couple of Japanese genii imparted to me through an interpreter two years ago as they described how they got live Caddis to stand still for their remarkable photographs. Then I might get one of these hyperactive creatures to pose long enough to be photographed on some red or yellow fall foliage.

We have come to the end of this book, and already there is unfinished business on the agenda for a future edition! Perhaps that is the best illustration I can leave: the opportunity for discovery is unlimited for an angler who independently chases hatches, using whatever methods, including the phenological flora-fauna method described here. The category of super hatches will never be closed to the fly-fisher who uses and observes nature as a guide to great fishing.

12

USEFUL FURTHER READING

Arbona Jr., Fred L. *Mayflies: The Angler and the Trout.* Tulsa: Winchester Press, 1980.

Caucci, Al and Bob Nastasi. *Hatches.* New York: Compara-hatch, Ltd., n.d.

Flick, Art. *Art Flick's New Streamside Guide.* New York: Crown and Toronto: General Books, 1969.

Hafele, Rick and Dave Hughes. *The Complete Book of Western Hatches.* Portland: Frank Amato Publications, n.d.

Juracek, John and Craig Mathews. *Fishing Yellowstone Hatches.* West Yellowstone: Blue Ribbon Flies, 1992.

LaFontaine, Gary. *Caddisflies.* New York: Nick Lyons Books, 1981.

Meck, Charles and Greg Hoover. *Great Rivers—Great Hatches.* Harrisburg: Stackpole, 1992.

Merrit, R.W. and K.W. Cummins. *An Introduction to the Aquatic Insects of North America.* Dubuque: Kendall/Hunt, 1978.

Richards, Carl, Doug Swisher and Fred L. Arbona Jr. *Stoneflies.* New York: Nick Lyons/Winchester Press, 1980.